CENTERED

Marking Your Map in A Muddled World

Dale Jenkins

ISBN-13: 978-1519141613

Cover & Layout: Joey Sparks
Professional editing: Kathy Jarrell

Published by The Jenkins Institute

thejenkinsinstitute.com

This material was originally written as material for Maywood Christian Camp in Hamilton, AL.

I dedicate this book solely to the memory of my Dad. The impact of his life on all who knew him was overwhelming. He loved God, God's Family and lost Souls. He gave his life helping build up the Kingdom of Heaven. I will spend a lifetime striving to imitate him as he imitated Christ.

ACKNOWLEDGEMENTS & THANKS

I cannot let this book go out without some extra-large "Thank You's:"

Jeff Goff is the consummate camp man. I love camp and have gone all my life, but the excellence he brings to the table is a cut above any in that field I have seen. His excellence in representing Maywood Christian Camp and in making it the best drives me to be better at the little I get to do.

Kathy Jarrell is better at my words than I am. The grace, speed, and exactness with which she does her work is second to none. She corrects my mistakes so much that I should probably list her as a co-author! Thank you.

Joey Sparks is a beast! He is Data. He is a "5 tool player"—preacher, publicist, encourager, writer, and brother! Thanks for your help, for the time you share with our work, but most of all for being a friend.

TABLE OF CONTENTS

INTRODUCTION

For most people there is a place that holds your heart. For some of us that place is deeply related to our faith. For me that place is Maywood Christian Camp in northwest Alabama.

What a blessing that place has been in my life. I've got a picture of me with my two brothers sitting on a log probably the first day they started clearing the property. I would have been two years old. That picture is over 50 years old now. It's there that I won my first competitive sport, a game of pingpong against Kevin Killingsworth. I learned to swim there. The first person I baptized was in that same pool where I learned to swim. I got my first kiss on those 80 acres...and got in big trouble for it. And I held my wife's hand for the first time walking down the main road into the camp. That was 34 years ago and I'm still holding her hand.

Let me share a story with you about one of the founders of that place. E.R. Bruce. My Dad (Jerry Jenkins) used to love to tell the story when Brother Bruce was present. Dad was preaching at Hamilton and Brother Bruce was preaching at Burleson. The land had already been promised by Brother Mays (Howard Mays, hence the name MAYwood). One bright sunny day dad and E.R. made their way out into the forest that would eventually become Maywood Christian Camp. There was no road and the terrain was rough. They made their way to the middle of an open field and stopped. Looking around and thinking of all the work and the cost to build there was somewhat overwhelming. We might say they were "counting the cost," when Brother Bruce said, "Jerry, can you hear that?" Dad thought there was some sort of wild animal out there. He said, "What?" Brother

Bruce said, "Listen." Dad listened hard and heard nothing. Brother Bruce said, "Listen harder. Jerry, can't you just hear the voices of the children playing?" He had a dream and worked toward that place becoming a mecca for Christians.

One phrase, attributed to Brother Bruce, appeared on the front of the Maywood Christian Camp book for most of the next 50 years: "Maywood Christian Camp: The Center of God's Universe."

I don't know how many people have told me over and over how Maywood is where they go to get re-energized, re-focused, or as Brother Bruce might like to hear it worded: **re-centered**. We need "centering" places. So as we study together "Centered," I pray that it is a blessing to you.

Where you are is the Center of your universe, and because of His great love for you, therefore the center of God's Universe.

CHAPTER 1

The Center of our Faith:
Christ
Colossians 1:13-20

The Center of our Faith: Christ
Read: Colossians 1:13-20

There weren't any diamond studded unicorns, the sky did not open, and I didn't discover the pot at the end of the rainbow; BUT it was, nonetheless, one of those ministry changing moments. I'm not sure if he heard it somewhere else or came up with it on his own but I was listening to one of my favorite preachers, David Shannon, preaching to preachers about preaching. He said: "The measure of a sermon is how long it is in the lesson before Jesus shows up...how long before you bring Christ into the sermon."

So before we take even a baby step forward, let's be clear. Without Jesus we don't even have a reason to think about our lives having center, gravity, or order. In fact, I suspect the prime reason most people's lives go askew is either that they never knew Christ or only knew Him casually.

We could ask David's question in other ways: How long in your morning is it before Jesus shows up in your thoughts? How long is it into your crisis before you turn to Jesus? How long is it in your heartache, heartbreak, heart attack, headache, or head game before you give it to the Lord?

In one of his best-sellers Paul wrote: "He is the beginning, the firstborn from the dead, that in everything he might be preeminent" (Colossians 1:18). And later in that same opening: "If then you have been raised with Christ, seek the things that are above, where Christ is, seated at the right hand of God...your life is hidden with Christ in God..." (3:1-3). A familiar kids' song paraphrases those thoughts, "I'm all wrapped up, I'm all tied up, I'm all tangled up with Jesus."

How long before Christ shows up?

He is on every page of your Bible. He's the ram in the bush, the feet in the fire, the stranger in the house, the Shepherd who is good, and the fountain that is pure.

His promise is true (remember, He can't lie —Titus 1:2), He will never leave you (Hebrews 13:5), and He will be with you (Matthew 28:18-20).

In your day "the risen Lord has gone before you" (Mark 14:28). There is no need to fear, where you are going He's already there (Proverbs 15:3; Colossians 1:17).

He ever lives to intercede for you (Hebrews 7:25).

He's looking for a fight with the one who would destroy you and when He calls it "over," it will be over before you can imagine (2 Thessalonians 2:8). He is the defender of His own.

You cannot lean on Him too heavily (Isaiah 41:13). He is our rock (Psalm 118:22; Matthew 21:42; Acts 4:11; 1 Peter 2:7) and the church's foundation (1 Corinthians 3:11; Ephesians 2:20).

He is the pioneer of our faith (Hebrews 12:1-2).

He is Alpha and Omega, beginning and end (Revelation 1:7-8).

He is the purpose behind the Old Testament (John 5:39). He is the reason the Jewish race was blessed (Genesis 12:1-3).

With Paul we emphasize, "I am determined to know nothing among you but Jesus Christ and Him crucified" (1 Corinthians 2:2).

If Christ is at the center of our lives then all else will fall in place. We cannot enter into a study called "Centered" without the confession that Jesus Christ is the Son of God and the Center of any discussion about faith and living for God.

In the words of one of my heroes, Jim Bill McInteer, back in 1976, "I believe we need people to inspire us to do more—more than just the formal contact with truth, I need somebody else who believes it, who lives it and who loves it to touch me and to help me down that journey of life." We all do. That is why "the Word became flesh" (John 1:14) so that "We have a chief priest who is able to sympathize with our weaknesses. He was tempted in every way that we are, but he didn't sin " (Hebrews 4:17).

Discussion:

Each lesson except this one will have a section called 13 Good Questions. This week we only have one question because this question is too big to have more than one!

1. How can you make Christ MORE the Center of your life Monday through Saturday?

CHAPTER 2

Centered on God
Psalm 19:1-4a; Romans 10:17

CHAPTER 5

Centered on God: Creation
Read: Psalm 19:1-4a; Romans 10:17

I want to talk to you about Faith and Belief in God, but this is going to be different. With apologies to Kyle Butt, Josh McDowell, Ralph Gilmore and others whose minds defy explanation (I'm truly amazed, and my faith grows every time I hear them teach), this lesson isn't going to be heavy on apologetics for two reasons:

1. There are a lot of us out here who don't have deep scientific brains; though I'm thankful beyond words for those who do and use them for His glory.

2. There are a billion questions the most educated atheist nor the most intellectual

Christian can't answer. Your beliefs are a decision. Stack all the books written by all the geniuses and visit all the websites. Ingest all you can. That stuff is fascinating and faith building, BUT at some point it comes down to a decision. Do I believe? Remember, we are asked to have "FAITH."

IT'S CALLED FAITH

I don't know how many people over the years I've talked with who were struggling because some person, event, or circumstance was causing them to doubt.

Lean in and listen closely: don't let it worry you if you have doubt. After all, it's called *Faith*. It's not called *Sight*. Sight comes later. There's plenty this side of eternity to cause the strongest person to question.

Faith is not about who can present the most well-constructed unanswerable argument. It is about a decision to believe one thing or another. Now, I know that decision has to be based upon something, but at some point one has to just decide whether to believe or not.

While doubt can be dangerous, it is not a sin to doubt. When you doubt, you join a host of good folks.

Thomas (of course, "Doubting" was his first name): He missed the first Sunday night meeting of the Followers when Jesus showed up (I'd remind you that Jesus still does shows up every time His People are together. Matthew 18:20) Thomas missed it and doubted it (John 20:25). Notice he didn't miss the next Sunday night and Jesus showed up again BUT notice, Jesus didn't punish Thomas for doubting. He offered proof for him...and for us (John 20:29b).

John the Baptist: We call Stephen the first Christian martyr (and we're not wrong, see Acts 7) but the first to die for preaching Christ was John the baptizer. He's in prison for preaching righteousness and sent some of his disciples to ask Jesus if He was really the Messiah or not (Luke 7:19). Amazing, here is the "forerunner" of Christ, the one who baptized Jesus, a mere man who interacted with God the Father, the Son and the Holy Spirit, and yet he has doubt. But Jesus didn't punish him for his doubt, He answered it (vs. 20-22). And a few verses later he says, "among those born of women there is not a greater prophet than John the Baptist" (vs. 28).

Then there's Mark 9:24. A father brought his son who had a severe sickness to Jesus. He has seen Jesus heal folks, he saw the actual power of Jesus in a miracle done right in front of his face yet he still says: "Lord, I believe, help my unbelief..." Jesus did not rebuke him, instead He healed the son.

FAITH IS NOT MIRACULOUS

Everyone has faith! When you turn on a light switch it is a matter of faith. Few of you could explain why or exactly how electricity works but when you flip that switch you still expect...light! You have faith. The question is when it comes to the important things of life where do YOU put your faith?

If you have faith in God, there is a reason. And if you put your faith in someone or something else, there is a reason. While it is "faith and not sight," it is not blind faith. Do you know you can grow your faith? Romans 10:17 says: "So then faith comes by hearing, and hearing by the word of God." Teacher, farmer, nurse, accountant, can I ask you a question? How is your faith? If it's weak and wishy-washy, I want to ask what you are feeding it? Are you feeding your faith the Word of God. If you are, your faith cannot help but grow. If you are not reading the Bible and meditating on it, then it's a guarantee you'll be constantly doubting and continually floundering. Listen. It really is that simple.

IT'S THE FIRST STEP

Most of us have heard what many call "the plan of salvation." Sometimes we rush to things like confession and repentance to get to baptism too quickly. Really you have to determine to believe or determine to disbelieve. And faith equals belief. When you determine to believe in God and in Christ as His Son, it changes how you see everything. It's denying God and Jesus as His Son that gets you in trouble.

Many of you have heard this question right before baptism at your home church, during a Gospel Meeting or Revival, at a Christian Camp or some other event, "Do you believe with all of your heart that Jesus Christ is the Son of God?" It is on that confessed belief that you are baptized into Christ. But it all starts with belief—a *decision* to *believe*.

We won't be deceptive about this at all. We want you to grow in your faith. Some of you may be thinking about being baptized. Some of you need to make that decision. We want, yes, WANT, you to act on that faith and make that decision. It's time to act on your faith.

WHAT ABOUT "THEM?"

Before I close this lesson I want to talk to you about one more thing. You were blessed. You have parents, friends, or someone in your life who is a Christian and you came to know about Christ—why? I don't know. But I do know God has a plan. And I do know you get to choose. You were blessed. NOW you get to determine how to use those blessings. What about those who don't have opportunity? I want you to know that they don't exist! If anyone wants to hear the gospel, God will see that His message gets to them. (We, Christians, are the vehicle He uses to spread His Good News. Matthew 28; Mark 16; Luke 24; Acts 1). Acts 17:27 says in part "so that they should seek the Lord, in the hope that they might grope for Him and find Him, though He is not far from each one of us." God is not far from any of us. (Read the whole context of that one). He has written in the universe that He is God, "The heavens declare the glory of God; And the firmament shows His handiwork. Day unto day utters speech, And night unto night reveals knowledge. There is no speech nor language Where their voice is not heard. Their line has gone out through all the earth, and their words to the end of the world" (Psalm 19:1-4). And Romans 1:20: "For since the creation of the world His invisible attributes are clearly seen, being understood by the things that are made, even His eternal power and Godhead, so that they are without excuse." I don't pretend to understand how, but if one seeks to know God, God will find a way to get His message to him (see Acts 10:1-4). But that's not your problem. The better question is WHAT ABOUT YOU? You have the Message. Are you ready to center your faith in it?

13 GOOD QUESTIONS
(To Answer and Discuss)

1. According to Hebrews 11:1 what is faith?

2. Why is faith not blind faith?

3. Who else believes there is one God (James 2:19)?

4. In what way/s can you strengthen your faith in God?

5. At what point could our doubt become dangerous?

6. What two components of faith must we have if our faith is to be described as pleasing?

7. Name something in nature that fortifies your faith in God and explain why?

8. List some Bible verses that help you in times of doubt.

9. What Biblical story of faith is your favorite (most inspiring to you) and why?

10. Will faith cause you to act on or obey God's command? Explain. Give examples.

11. Because of Abraham's faith, what was he called?

12. What types of questions have you been asked by friends who doubt God?

13. What is the best way to handle these situations?

CHAPTER 3

Centered on You
Luke 15; 1 Corinthians 12;
Romans 12:3-6

Centered on You

Read: Luke 15; 1 Corinthians 12;
Romans 12:3-6

I bet you have somebody in your life who is an awesome story teller. They are great creatively at making stories come to life or excellent at re-telling an event to make you feel like you were there. Most of us love a great story!

A GREAT STORY HAS A GREAT START

""There was once a man who was going down from Jerusalem to Jericho when robbers attacked him, stripped him, and beat him up..." (Luke 10).

A wealthy man hired servants and went away... (Matthew 21).

Ten virgins were invited to a wedding feast.... (Matthew 25).

A farmer went out to his field... (Mark 4).

There was a poor widow and an uncaring judge... (Luke 18).

What you may have never considered is that Jesus is the greatest story teller who ever lived. He was the best there ever was or will be. I grew up with a page of Bible Definitions Dad and Mom used to help us. One of them was:

PARABLE = An earthly story with a heavenly meaning

Dr. Luke writes about three of Jesus' best stories (Luke 15). The first went something like this. A shepherd had 100 sheep and one of them that wandered off. He left his 99 sheep and searched high and low for the one that was lost. When he found it, he called his friends and said celebrate with me! The second story is similar: There was a woman who had ten coins and lost one of them. She dropped everything and didn't stop looking 'till she found the coin. When she found it, she called her friends and said "Rejoice with me..." Charles Dickens (you know, the guy who wrote about Tiny Tim) called the third of these stories the greatest short story ever written. There was a dad who lost a son, and when the son returned, he threw the feast to end all feasts because his lost son was found.

These stories are touching—but why? It has to be the common elements. Something was lost, it was found, and there was joy. There's something neat (at least to me) in the first two stories that reveals the nature of God to us. Who cares about one lost coin when you have a pocketful? Who would care about one wandering sheep when 99% are still with you? I'll tell you who! God does!

Have you ever felt like a penny? ...not worth that much. Who cares if you are here are gone? ... one sheep among 100 ...not that important? But YOU need to hear this—**YOU are valuable to...GOD!** For more on this read John 14:6-11 and 2 Peter 3:9.

WHAT'S IT WORTH TO YOU?

We tend to place value on things based on: **Age**—newer is worth more than older unless you are talking about an antique then it's worth more. **Materials**—the Apple Watch Edition does absolutely nothing different than the Sport one that costs over $9500 less, it just has some gold in it. **Function**—If something works, makes our lives easier, or does something we like, we pay more for it. I'm not sure there is anything wrong with any of that. BUT when we transfer that to people, it is wrong. God does not value someone more because of age, abilities or wealth. He values people for the one thing that sets them apart from everything else—they/we have a soul.

Did you know there is a reason we oppose abortion? It really has nothing to do with baby killing. In fact we sympathize with those confused hurting people who feel they have no where to turn and so seek what they see as the simple way out—abortion. Get rid of the issue. But you see, the issue is really much bigger than if it's a baby or not. Any honest person in support of abortion today cannot deny that fact today. Here's the bigger issue, the sanctity of human life, any life, any human. God made us different than the rest of the animals. He made that clear in Genesis 2. We have a soul.

DON'T READ THIS

Now, I want to do something you never do in writing to young people. I want to reference a very old and very archaic song but a power filled one!

It was written by Charles Wesley in 1762 (exactly 200 years before I was born) and it is, uhhh, majestic. Wesley was studying the book of Leviticus one night and reading from a commentary written by Matthew Henry. Please read it slowly and don't dismiss it easily. He wrote:

A charge to keep I have,
A God to glorify,
A never-dying soul to save,
And fit it for the sky.

To serve the present age,
My calling to fulfill:
Oh, may it all my pow'rs engage
To do my Master's will!

IT TOOK A LONG TIME TO GET TO THE POINT BUT...

All the discussion about a soul doesn't really mean anything unless you think about what it means to you. If I really have a soul, what responsibilities does that give me? If I have a soul what does it mean about what I do with my time and how I live my life?

If I have a soul and it is a gift to me from God it gives meaning to living. That fact makes me worth something. It means my life and my service are BIG and important. It means to waste it, is a horrible misuse.

Let me be frank (which is odd because I'm Dale and not Frank), there are two things that really concern me for you:
1. The suicide rate has gone up.
2. The feeling of meaninglessness has also increased.

But, if you realize you have a soul and you believe it is from God, things change totally! Your life is suddenly very important. You do count. And you have a purpose beyond anything mere words can express. A purpose bigger than anything you can dream and even bigger than the 70 or 80 years you may spend on this little globe.

You are not a lost penny, or sheep or even a lost child! You, as a Christian have been found, bought, and given value by the God of the universe. You are not an accident or unwanted.

Today we want you to think about what God could do with your life if you were to make yourself totally and unreservedly available to Him.

"...God set the members every one of them in the body, as it hath pleased Him" (1 Corinthians 12:18).

"...God has dealt to each one a measure of faith. For as we have many members in one body, but all the members do not have the same function, so we, being many, are one body in Christ, and individually members of one another. Having then gifts differing according to the grace that is given to us, let us use them..." (Romans 12:3-6).

You have something to contribute. To not use your abilities for God, is to waste them: To not use your abilities for the glory of God, is to handicap the Body of Christ. Will you try? Will you begin to use your abilities for the very purpose for which you received them?

13 GOOD QUESTIONS
(To Answer and Discuss):

1. What is your favorite story Jesus told and why?

2. How do most people typically determine a person's worth? How should we determine a person's worth?

3. Why should we value life?

4. Why should we cast our cares upon God? (1 Peter 5:7).

5. What were the three lost things Jesus talked about in Luke 15?

6. Who places value on those who are lost?

7. Why does God value people above all other things?

8. According to Matt 16:26 what is more valuable than the whole world?

9. Why do you think we often believe others' talents are more valuable than our own?

10. What do you as a soul have to contribute to God's work?

11. List the talents God has given you which you could use in the church.

12. How could we help a friend who is struggling to find his/her value in the church?

13. Pick a friend and identify what special ability or gift they have that is useful to God. Then share that with him/her.

CHAPTER 4

Centered on Service
John 14:1-17

Centered on Service
Read: John 13:1-17

There's a song written by Tim Nichols and Craig Wiseman from a few years ago called "Live Like You Were Dying." Here are some of the lyrics:

"He said I was in my early 40's,
With a lot of life before me,
And a moment came that stopped me on a dime.
I spent most of the next days, lookin' at the x-rays,
Talkin' 'bout the options and talkin' 'bout sweet time.
Asked him when it sank in, that this might really be the real end.
How's it hit ya, when you get that kind of news.
Man what ya do.

And he says, I went sky divin',
I went rocky mountain climbin',
I went 2.7 seconds on a bull name Fumanchu.
And I loved deeper,
And I spoke sweeter,
And I gave forgiveness I've been denying,
And he said someday I hope you get the chance,
To live like you were dyin'.

He said I was finally the husband,
That most the time I wasn't.
And I became a friend a friend would like to have.
And all the sudden goin' fishing,
Wasn't such an imposition.
And I went three times that year I lost my dad.
Well I finally read the good book,
And I took a good long hard look at what I'd do
If I could do it all again.
And then.

For most folks who see the end coming on, living out the truly important, saying the most significant and finishing well becomes big. Well, never did anyone see his own time on earth ending like Jesus did. And, even with the Son of God it seems His words became more passionate and the mood became more about the urgent. His prayers for the disciples and us are passionate (John 14). And His actions? Well, He didn't go out and ride a bull or skydive (He invented bulls and had already been skydiving—only without a plane or parachute). No, His breath-taking thrill was of another sort. Read it yourself.

"...Jesus knew that his hour had come to depart out of this world to the Father, having loved his own who were in the world, he loved them to the end...knowing that the Father had given all things into his hands, and that he had come from God and was going back to God, rose from supper. He laid aside his outer garments, and taking a towel, tied it around his waist. Then he poured water into a basin and began to wash the disciples' feet and to wipe them with the towel that was wrapped around him...When he had washed their feet and put on his outer garments and resumed his place, he said to them, 'Do you understand what I have done to you? You call me Teacher and Lord, and you are right, for so I am. If I then, your Lord and Teacher, have washed your feet, you also ought to wash one another's feet. For I have given you an example, that you also should do just as I have done to you. Truly, truly, I say to you, a servant is not greater than his master, nor is a messenger greater than the one who sent him.

If you know these things, blessed are you if you do them" (John 13:1-17).

Jesus did what most folks do, He fulfilled life goals. It's just His focus was/is different than most folks. His fantasies and fulfillment came not from something that was self-serving, but from serving! Now, to be sure this was what we'd call a "teachable moment," but if we think the subject is dirty feet then we have missed the moment. Jesus is not enacting "foot washing" as a ceremonial tradition for Christians to follow. What the Lord is saying is that we have an obligation to meet the real, genuine needs of those around us. It's pretty simple—He washed their feet because their feet were dirty and that's what they needed, and also because it showed that He was a true servant doing what needed to be done and stepping to the dirtiest and most undesirable task. His point was, He would do anything to serve others. He would help in any way needed. He will prove this vibrantly hours later when He dies on the cross for their (and our) sins. But for now, He is setting an enduring and eternal example—one we best not miss: "I have given you an example, that you also should do just as I have done to you. Truly, truly, I say to you, a servant is not greater than his master."

Now this isn't the first time the Lord had tried to teach this to the Apostles. In Matthew 20:26 He said: "Jesus called them to Him and said, 'You know that the rulers of the Gentiles lord it over them, and their great ones exercise authority over them. It shall not be so among you. But whoever would be great among you must be your servant, and whoever would be first among you must be your slave, even as the Son of Man came not to be served but to serve, and to give His life as a ransom for many.'" In Mark 9:33: "And when He was in the house He asked them, 'What were you discussing on the way?' But they kept silent, for on the way they had argued with one another about who was the greatest. And He sat down and called the twelve. And He said to them, 'If anyone would be first, he must be last of all and servant of all.'" We might say they didn't get it and that we still don't. But I'd rather just say this is a very hard lesson to learn. It is human nature to want to be served BUT it is godly to want to serve.

So we should be in the business of finding opportunities in life to "wash each others feet," to serve each other in ways that are real (meet real needs) and that others would not be willing to do. We should stretch ourselves to go beyond the easy. We should visibly challenge ourselves to find ways to serve.

In 1978 Jimmy and Carol Owens published "The Servant Song" that we sing today:

Make me a servant Lord, make me like You
For You are a servant, make me one, too.
Make me a servant, do what You must do
To make me a servant, make me like You.

GOD MADE YOU

And He made you to be a servant. Hebrews 10:24 says "Let us think of ways to motivate one another to acts of love and good works" (NLT).

Ephesians 2:10 makes it even clearer: "For we are his workmanship, created in Christ Jesus for good works, which God prepared beforehand, that we should walk in them." That word "workmanship" is an interesting word. It is used six times in the Old Testament. Each time it refers to the skill and the crafts of those who designed the gold decorations of Solomon's temple. Great care and effort went into who would do that work and then into the work itself. The word is only used once in the New Testament. There it refers to YOU, Christian. You are the very work of God to be put on display before the world to show His skill. And how do you do it? Created "for love and good works," you do it by being a loving servant. You are God's work of art before your school, community, sports team, cheer squad, and lunch room group, to show off His craft by serving them! Now, that's a thing of beauty. You count!

God did not save any of us to sit on the sideline and watch, but to serve. We were saved to serve not to sit. In Paul's inspired and inspiring words to the church he said: " For just as the body is one and has many members, and all the members of the body, though many, are one body, so it is with Christ. For in one Spirit we were all baptized into one body...the body does not consist of one member but of many. If the foot should say, 'Because I am not a hand, I do not belong to the body,' that would not make it any less a part of the body. And if the ear should say, 'Because I am not an eye, I do not belong to the body,' that would not make it any less a part of the body. If the whole body were an eye, where would be the sense of hearing? If the whole body were an ear, where would be the sense of smell? But as it is, **God arranged the members in the body, each one of them, as He chose.** ...As it is, there are many parts, yet one body" (1 Corinthians 12:12-20 emp: dj).

So, what are you doing as a member of the Body? Where are you serving? To not do so, handicaps the Body. You are not to become a servant when you hit age 22 or when you get married or when you have a job BUT when you are baptized into Christ. I want to challenge you to start today doing something GREAT—finding small and big ways to serve for Christ. Imagine this powerful truth, YOU have the privilege and opportunity to partner with God! You get to be in His entourage! You get to be a part of what God is doing in the world today. WOW! What a thrill!

Back to our Tim McGraw ballad we began with. Near the end he sings:
Like tomorrow was a gift and you've got eternity
To think about what you do with it,
What could you do with it, what can
I do with with it, what would I do with it.

You know you are dying. Today is a gift, what will you DO with it?

13 GOOD QUESTIONS
(To Answer and Discuss):

1. What was Jesus Teaching as he washed the Disciples' feet?

2. When are we most like Jesus?

3. Look at Philippians 2:5-11. What about these verses stand out to you in regards to the degree that Jesus served others?

4. Paul was a servant for whose sake? 2 Corinthians 4:5.

5. How did Isaiah respond to God? Isaiah 6:8.

6. How does Jesus say you can become the greatest (reach your true potential)?

7. For what purpose are we created in Christ Jesus?

8. What is someone who commits sin? See John 8:34

9. In what way/s have you served God in the past month? What are you doing for God and/or others?

10. If you were to describe your association with the church as a body part, which body part would you be?

11. How do we develop the "heart of a servant?" What does that phrase mean?

12. At your age, what are some ways you can serve at home, in the church, in our communities?

13. Think about some ways your service could help aid a missionary in the United States or overseas.

CHAPTER 5

Centered on Church
Matthew 16:16-18; Titus 2:10;
1 Peter 3:3-4

Centered on Church

Read: Matthew 16:16-18; Titus 2:10;

1 Peter 3:3-4

If you are reading this (and obviously you are) you are possibly a Millennial or from Generation Z. Just like always, things are changing. One thing that is certain is change.

We're living in a good time and a bad time. Yep, it's a bad time. The morals in our country continue to deteriorate. Divorce, breaking of the vows made before God and ignoring His plan of one man and one woman for life, seems to have become the accepted norm. Tolerance of homosexuality has swept our country faster than any societal change in the history of humanity. You can't watch a single prime time network TV show without hearing words that are godless and jokes that belittle all that is holy and good. Lying and cheating no longer shock us in our government, police departments, businesses and schools. Some folks get all worked up about that. We shouldn't be. God said: "But evil people and charlatans will go from bad to worse" (2 Timothy 3:13 NET). I'm not a pessimist or an optimist, I'm a believer in what God says. I love to see people do good and bless other's lives. Regardless of how bad things are around you, you still have that opportunity. Christians would do well to be reminded that a: there is no such thing as a Christian nation and b: Christianity was born into a much more pagan culture than the one we live in today.

Some folks are just as down on the church as they are on society.* (page 82) They are convinced the church is going away, dying, irrelevant, and just plain out of style.

SURE COULD USE A LITTLE GOOD NEWS TODAY!

The fact is, future looks very good.

"... I will build my church; and the gates of hell shall not prevail against it" (Matthew 16:18, Jesus).

"... the God of heaven set up a kingdom, which shall never be destroyed: and the kingdom shall not be left to other people, but it shall break in pieces and consume all these kingdoms, and it shall stand for ever" (Daniel 2:44).

"Then comes the end, when he delivers the kingdom to God the Father after destroying every rule and every authority and power" (1 Corinthians 15:24).

Now to be sure, congregations come and go as areas change, communities age, or leadership becomes stagnant or weak, but the church, the church of our Lord, the church of Christ, isn't going anywhere, but forward. There is reason for concern in places and situations. Some seem to want to toss the Text aside and "do church" their way instead of God's way. Others seem to want to worship the past with its traditions and ways of doing things more than God and His Way of doing things. The church is going to be just fine. We have God's Promise on that and He "can't lie" (Titus 1:2).

IT GETS MUCH MORE EXCITING THAN THAT THOUGH

In fact there is a lot of reason to be excited about what is happening among spiritually minded people in our own culture. Every generation (yes, even Millennial's and Z'ers) seem to be tiring of denominationalism and the hierarchy that goes with it.

It is therefore not shocking that what are known as "mainline" denominations are dying with blinding speed! The Methodist church is losing nearly 100,000 members every year. Since the year 2000 the Presbyterian church has lost roughly a million members, over 30%

of its total membership. The Episcopal church boasted 4 million members in 1992, the most recent data shows weekly attendance at around 500,000.** (page 82) Now that is both bad and good news. It's bad news because traditionally the mainline denominational people of our culture helped our cities and communities be better, more moral places. It's good news because it is a sign that younger people are rejecting man's religious rules and in the process many are favoring more "organic church." AND, while we may not have done as good a job at it as we wish, it is true that we do not want to be a denomination and "organic" Christianity is what we have been trying to spread for a long time. What we are at our heart is what a younger generation is searching for.

How about this concept: toss aside any belief, idea, concept, practice of faith, action, tradition that the Bible does not command or authorize and just be Christians. Here's what's awesome. It is what the church of Christ has always been. In fact when we cease to be that, we ought to take His name off the sign.

There's nothing new here, in fact it's something very old; we call it simple New Testament Christianity. The concept is both beautiful and godly. Any individual can pick up the Bible and learn for himself simply by reading and following what to do to "make God happy." He/she can in fact: Become a Christian like the Bible says, worship like the Bible says and live like the Bible says.

The rise of community churches is simply a reaction of people getting tired of religious politics. Some of them make a move in the right direction. Though sometimes not far enough. Can we bear some of the blame for not being clear enough and present enough to commend them and encourage those good steps? Are we majoring in junk instead of Gospel and seen as people who argue and defend rather than teach and baptize. The biggest weakness of these churches seems to be that they give people only what they want —which is a nice marketing ploy—but how about determining to forget self and give God what He wants? "You will seek me and find me, when you seek me with all your heart" (Jeremiah 29:13). "If you love me, you will do what I command" (John 14:15, Jesus).

MORE GOOD NEWS

The Gospel still works (Romans 1:16). We see it all the time when people get out and share this Good News. The issue isn't the power of God or the Message of God but whether or not we make an effort to actually tell that life-giving story. 1 Peter 3:15 instructs: "...but in your hearts honor Christ the Lord as holy, always being prepared to make a defense to anyone who asks you for a reason for the hope that is in you; yet do it with gentleness and respect." Some have slightly twisted this text (I believe honestly so) and have left the impression that we have to be able to answer any question or that it is a verse about Christian Apologetics. While we would obviously not oppose all godly scholarship we would also discourage any misuse of the text. The verse actually teaches we are to be able to prepared to defend our "hope." Can you tell another about why you have hope in Christ? About your salvation? About God's grace? Then do it. That is God's growth plan for His Kingdom! And, it works.

There are people in your life, your school, on your team, at your work, in your social circles who need the Gospel. This is an amazing thing. You don't have to be creative, or sly, or gifted with great words—you just tell them how you obeyed the Gospel. And here is what is beautiful: Any century, any country, any person, any age, shake it up and pour it out, and it comes out the same! The Word is the same for all when it comes to being God's Person.

WHAT'S THE BIG DEAL?

Why all this talk about church anyway? I
mean, isn't one just as good as another? It's
Christ and believing in Him that is
important, right? Well, obviously it is Christ
that is important, but that is precisely WHY
the church is important. He promised to
build His church (Matthew 16:16-18), so it
belongs to Him. He died for it to come in to
existence (Acts 20:28). The church is His Body
on earth today (Colossians 1:18). And when
someone comes to believe in Him, it is the
Lord who at that point of obedience adds
them to the church (Acts 2:41). To say all that
is not exceptionally significant would be just
ludicrous. That is WHY the church is
important. And that is why HE gets to decide
what we do as the church, in the church. That
is why HE gets to "set the rules." And that is

why we had better be very careful about not obeying His commands (John 14:15). I want to be clear, I love the church and would never want to do anything in any way to harm the bride of Christ (Ephesians 5:25-27).

ONE MORE THING—YOUR PART

Your writer is a preacher. I've preached in a lot of places and noticed something very neat. Every community that I've been in, there is that person, Ron or Joe or Sara or Charles who lives such a Christlike life, who so serves and loves and lives that people see them as a person they both admire and wish to live like. That person is my hero. They are the ones whose name can get you into any house or heart to study the Gospel with others. It doesn't matter how damaged the name or reputation of the church is, you say the name

Ron Davis and you get an immediate hearing. So, what if **you** became that person whose life so "beautifies the Gospel" (Titus 2:10; 1 Peter 3:3-4) that people are opened to the Good News because of your influence?

Now, what does that have to do with a lesson on the church? You probably already know, the church is not the building it is the people! You are the church! What people think of church is defined by what Christians think of the church and what people think of Christ is often determined by what people think of His church—the Christian. If Christianity isn't making you a better person shouldn't we remove the "Christ" part of that term? Be a positive impact on the church with your life and outlook—be centered.

* I'd rather not bring you in on some of the struggles of the church—but with the internet and some of the attitudes of those involved—it won't be long for any of you until you are affected in some way by these things. There have always been those who did harm with their words and actions—proving a lack of love for the church and hurting those around them (1 Timothy 1:19; 1:4).

** Sadly the patterns that are leading some of the "mainline denominations" to their demise are the failed practices and patterns that some who have given up on simple New Testament Christianity are suggesting and adapting.

13 GOOD QUESTIONS
(To Answer and discuss)

1. What is the Church?

2. What is another term for the church (Matthew 16: 18,19)?

3. Who is the head of the church (Ephesians 5:23)? With what did Christ obtain the church (Acts 20:28)?

4. What is the church called in 1 Tim 3:15?

5. Why is the church is so important to God?

6. Discuss the beauty of New Testament Christianity.

7. Tradition or Commandment? (Circle the ones that are not traditions):

Partaking the Lord's Supper on Sunday?

A cappella singing for worship to God?

Two worship services on Sunday?

Marriage between a man and a woman?

Wednesday night Bible study?

Baptism for the remission of sins?

Giving our money on the 1st Day of the week?

Having a certain song leader?

Using unleavened bread and fruit of the vine for the Lord's Supper

Having Bible class on Sunday morning.

8. What great news can you share about the church to others?

9. Why is the church going forward?

10. Discuss value of giving God what He wants.

11. How could the decline in numbers of people joining denominational churches be a potentially positive thing for us evangelistically?

12. Share an example where you have seen the Gospel still at work today.

13. Name some ways you can help keep the reputation of the church a positive one.

CHAPTER 6

Centered on Faithfulness
Hebrews 12:1-3

Centered on Faithfulness
Read: Hebrews 12:1-3

This last lesson will be a little shorter—I want you to reserve time to think back over these lessons. If in a group, talk about them. But before we go I want to to talk with you about something I'm passionate about this. I hope you leave this study on a spiritual high. That's what I love most about writing. It can cause people to believe and to dream of what God can do with them. I love that each week people fall in love with Jesus and His People. I love that people obey the Gospel. I love that people can renew and recommit, reconnect and rededicate.

But to be honest, there's something I don't like. I don't like that some of you will toss this little book aside. Put it in an old draw or chest and you'll toss your faith in with it to be stored away. I don't like that some of you opened your heart in Bible class but close it up with the church doors on Sunday evening. I don't like that some of you who opened your mouth and sung sung "Oh, How I Love Jesus" but will live like you don't know Him the rest of the week. And I don't like that some of you who use that tongue to praise God will use it to curse others a few days from now.

What your teacher wants, and your classmates teacher want, what your preacher wants and your elders want, and most of all what your God wants is for this to be the beginning of a daily commitment to Him.

So how do I live a life Centered on Faithfulness?

REMEMBER WHAT FAITHFULNESS IS
Revelation gives us what can be a scary instruction: "Be faithful unto death, and I will give you the crown of life" (Revelation 2:10). That's big and I would never want to

minimize it but I also want you to understand that the word "Faithful" does not mean "Perfect." God does not say "be perfect unto death" because you cannot (Romans 3:23). If you could be perfect there would be no need for Christ's death. 1 John 1 says we are to "walk in the light" but a handful of verses later John says that when we do sin we have Jesus there for us (1 John 2:1). Let me illustrate. If you were to ask my wife if I am a perfect husband she would laugh at the thought—but if you ask her if I'm a faithful husband she would assure you that I am.

REALIZE THAT IT WON'T BE EASY

Have you ever run a 50-meter dash? Yeah, and you were timed too. It may have been a challenge but 99% of you did complete it. You never considered quitting—after all it was just 50 meters. How about a marathon? Have you run one? 99% of you have not. I have and I want to tell you, after about mile 15 (of 26.2) there was some point in every mile that I wanted to stop running. The Bible talks about the Christian life being a race, and it would be pretty simple if it was a 50 meter dash but it's not, it's an endurance race—more of a marathon (Hebrews 12:1-3). If you leave camp thinking it will be just as easy "out there" as it is "here," you are allowing yourself to be deceived. You are going out from here into a place where doing right is more likely to be mocked than applauded. But that is where you will live MOST of your life. LOVE the times when we get to be together—camp, worship, conferences, rallies. If you think this marathon of the Christian life is simple, you'll never finish but the victory is worth effort.

RECOGNIZE THAT YOU CAN DO THIS

While it is not easy you need to hear this important truth: *God never asks us to do that which is beyond our ability to do!*

Here's a verse to put on your mirror and read every morning when you brush your teeth: "God is faithful. He will not allow the temptation to be more than you can stand. When you are tempted, he will show you a way out so that you can endure" (1 Corinthians 10:13). There is always, 100% of the time a way out of the temptation! God will hold satan back from tempting you above what YOU can handle. That's powerful! Own that verse and win.

Can I give you some tools? Some amazingly simple-to-use tools to finishing this marathon! Don't think I'm toying with you—these tools have been the key to faithfulness for every person who has been faithful to the Lord for 2000 years and they will help you:

Pray about everything all the time! Talk to God about your struggles and your worries, about everything.

Read His Word! Don't just talk to Him, let Him talk back to you. Nothing will make your spiritual life stronger than time spent in the Word of God.

Worship! When God's People get together you be there with them. You will gain and give strength to others. Support and be supported by these people called the church.

REALIZE YOU'RE NOT ALONE

You have allies. There are friends who are wanting to go to heaven just like you! Be open and honest with them. Encourage and be encouraged. Communicate that you need them to help you. The whole concept of church is a community of saved people supporting each other.

You have an Ally. More than just brothers and sister you have Jesus as your Savior. He will never leave you or forsake you. In fact look at the text (Hebrews 12:2) "Looking unto Jesus." There are a billion things satan will toss your direction to distract your gaze, from doubt and distrust to depression and disillusion. But continue in; the midst of any obstacle to keep your attention turned on the Lord, and you will be OK.

May God's richest blessing be yours!

13 GOOD QUESTIONS
(To Answer and discuss)

1. They that wait upon the Lord will run and not be what?(Isaiah 40:31).

2. What is laid up for those who have kept the faith? (2 Timothy 4:7,8).

3. Who would you say is the most faithful, godly person you know?

4. How often does God provide a way of escaping temptations?

5. When does the Scripture say that God will leave you or forsake you?

6. What is faithfulness?

7. Why is faithfulness not easy?

8. Name 3 tools God has given us to help us be faithful.

9. Discuss how being faithful does not mean being perfect.

10. Name some ways you can strengthen your Bible study habits at home.

11. Make a list of the friends you have whom you need to talk to about Jesus and plan to do that when you return home.

12. Make a plan to study with someone who will help you grow consistently after you go home.

13. Share contact info with each other in class (cell numbers/email addresses): Help each other BE FAITHFUL all through life!

OTHER BOOKS FROM The Jenkins Institute

All I Ever Wanted to Do Was Preach by Dale Jenkins
Before I Go compiled by Jeff and Dale Jenkins
5 Habits and A Decision by Dale Jenkins
A Mother's Heart by Jeff and Dale Jenkins
A Father's Heart by Jeff and Dale Jenkins
A Youth Minister's Heart by Dale Jenkins
You and Me and the People in the Pew by Tracy Moore
The Glory of Preaching by Clarence Deloach and Jay
Lockhart

OTHER BOOKS WE HAVE BEEN A PART OF
Thoughts from the Mound by Jeff Jenkins
Seeking True Unity edited by Dale Jenkins
God's Plan for Unity (Bible study workbook) by Jeff Jenkins
A Minister's Heart by Dale Jenkins
Redeeming the Times edited by Jeff Jenkins
Reaching for Passion edited by Jeff Jenkins

for ordering information:
visit TheJenkinsInstitute.com or
email TheJenkinsInstitute@gmail.com

Made in the USA
Monee, IL
09 March 2021